James Cutbush

Edgar F. Smith

Contents

PREFACE 7
JAMES CUTBUSH AN AMERICAN CHEMIST 1788-1823 8

JAMES CUTBUSH

BY

Edgar F. Smith

TO
MY FELLOW-CHEMISTS

PREFACE

There is nothing thrilling in the following pages. They contain the story of the life-work of a very modest man deeply interested in and enamoured with the science of chemistry, who sought also to inspire others and to familiarize the general public of his time with the intimate connection of chemistry with manufactures and things which enter so largely into every-day occupations. He was an active member of a small group of chemists who, in the early years of eighteen hundred, caused thousands of the laity to give thought to the possibilities of Chemistry, and in addition was a pioneer in pyrotechnics, on which account he is deservedly entitled to every recognition. More than a century has passed since his most serious efforts were put forth. However, it will not be long until that early galaxy of chemical enthusiasts of which he was a member will be accorded a high place in the history of the development of the science in America.

JAMES CUTBUSH
AN AMERICAN CHEMIST
1788-1823

It is scarcely conceivable that anything pertaining to the development of chemical science in America would fail to interest its chemists. The response to the needs of the Nation in the last few years has shown how marvelously they wrought and the wonderful things which they brought to light. Yet in the long ago--in the days of which we only know by hearsay, and through desultory reading, there lived chemists with enthusiasm, knowledge and initiative, whose aim it was to have their chosen science contribute to the welfare of humanity. In the labors of such men as James Woodhouse, Robert Hare, Adam Seybert, Henry Seybert, John Redman Coxe, Joseph Cloud, Gerard Troost, and many others, the scientific spirit predominated, although with it went the purpose, more or less sharply defined, of making their acquirements useful. Particularly noticeable was this in the instance of Woodhouse.

The general consensus of opinion among present-day chemists is that chemistry should be helpful to all. It may and should be scientific, but its principles ought to be scientifically applied in every useful manner.

The reader, desirous of learning the aims and ambitions of the fathers of the science in our country, will profit by turning to the files of the *Aurora*, an old daily paper of Philadelphia, for the year 1808, and beginning about the middle of July will there encounter a most interesting series of articles on the applications of chemistry under the general heading

APPLICATION OF CHEMISTRY TO ARTS AND MANUFACTURES

There are fifteen separate papers. In considering the period--1808,--the age of the young Republic, and that the times were far from quiet; that unrest and uncertainty prevailed as to the fate of the Republic, it does not surprise that thought should have been given to means of protection; hence gunpowder was the very first product to engage the author of the series of articles. The proving and analysis of the powder are discussed at length. The methods appear very primitive in the light of present-day knowledge, but one must not forget the period. One hundred years hence the masterpieces of present-day chemists will perhaps provoke smiles upon the countenances of those who perchance read them. In this pioneer contribution on gunpowder analysis the charcoal of the powder is often called "oxid of carbon." In referring to the separation of potassium and sodium it is recommended to precipitate out the first in the form of tartrate. Naturally, nitre itself comes in for serious thought and the explosibility of the mixture of charcoal, nitre and sulphur arrests the author's attention, for he emphasizes the fact--

> "that, independent of the formation of gases or airs, the agency of caloric, or matter of heat, generated in the process of combustion, considerably facilitates the strength of the powder, in consequence of producing the expansion of these airs."

Recently, under the pressure of a national necessity, which will not soon be forgotten, the problem of getting nitre--nitrates and kindred bodies--had the earnest attention of chemists. So, in the period before and after 1808, methods of forming nitre had grave consideration. For instance, this question, now amusing, was propounded--

> "How much nitre could be manufactured from the refuse animal and vegetable matter of the City of Philadelphia in case of emergency? What quantity could be prepared by elixating or washing the rubbish of old buildings, the earth of stables, cellars, etc., and the soil of certain tracts of the United States?"

It is quite proper that mention should have also been made of the natural *nitre beds*, as well as of the artificial beds built up from slow experience. Reference is made that in France nitre was won from the lime and rubbish of old, ruinous buildings, and from the floors of stables and pigeon houses, while it is also recorded that during the American Revolution, the

> "same means, by the hand of economy and industry, afforded quantities of this article in certain of the then Colonies, and"

that in the Southern portions it was obtained from the earthen floors of tobacco houses.

The presentation of the earliest methods of getting nitre is extremely interesting, extended and elaborate, giving the reader a full view of pioneer conditions and endeavor. The scheme of purification of nitre for gunpowder use is illuminating and attractive. Attention is directed to the saltpetre rock and caves of the western portion of our country.

The preparation of charcoal is discussed. The adaptability of charcoal from various sources receives careful thought in connection with its use in gunpowder; so, too, the sulphur used for this particular purpose, and there is recommended as a source of this ingredient, the common pyrites so abundant throughout the States. Among other topics, of vital interest in these days, discussed in the continuing articles, is the manufacture of spirit from potatoes. The method employed in Germany is presented in detail after which it is said--

> "Potato spirit of excellent quality has been made in this city (Philadelphia). It is found, not only to be much cheaper than grain used entirely, but to afford better flavoured liquor and other qualities which give it a decided preference."

Fermentation, yeast and baking receive mention. Brewing and the different kinds of beer are fully examined. In those days adulteration was practiced, for wormwood and quassia were found as substitutes. The preparation of beer and ale for home consumption would very likely find little favor in the "dry-bone" spirit of the present, much less would the refining of wines and other spirituous liquors of high alcohol content meet with approbation. However, such prohibitory questions as are now discussed did not vitally concern our forefathers, so that it was most proper and praiseworthy to advise the public how, through the instrumentality of chemistry, many of the needed articles of life might be made in the highest degree of purity. In many homes there existed miniature brewing plants.

At the other extreme, among useful commodities, were the manufacture of fish glue, common glue, gelatine, albumen, magnesia alba, etc.

The several articles thus published in one of the most respected and influential papers of that early day--1808--had for their purpose the education of the general public in the application of a science to their use, but there was also a desire to arouse a deep and steady interest in science in general, which seems quite plain from a quotation from that remarkable address of Dr. John Morgan--at one time Physician-in-Chief of the American Army. The passage was--

> "Oh! let it never be said in this City or in this Province, so happy in its climate and in its soil, where Commerce has long flourished and plenty smiled, that science, the amiable daughter of liberty and sister of opulence, droops her languid head, or follows behind with a slow, unequal pace."

Doubtless deeply moved himself by this impassioned appeal, the author of the *Aurora* papers exclaimed--

> "I pronounce with confidence this shall never be the case. Every useful kind of learning shall here fix a favorite seat and shine forth in meredian splendour, to accomplish which may *every* heart and *every* hand be united."

And then, probably overpowered by an inner, compelling force and conscious of the possibilities of his science in the cause of man and the undeveloped resources of our country, quietly awaiting the oncoming alterations to be performed by applying chemistry, he continues with like spirit--

> "If ever there was a time to bring the Arts and Manufactures to perfection in this Country, it is the present; for the season is approaching, when, of necessity, which is the mother of invention, our internal resources, and the application of them to our wants, will advance a brilliant

and glorious epoch in the annals of our Country--second to none but the declaration of independence. Who is to establish the ***chain*** of manufactures--to convert the crude productions of Nature into useful articles; but you enlightened citizens, men of ***science*** and ***improvement***, ***artists*** and manufacturers. The laboratory of Nature will be thrown open to you, and to use the scriptural phrase, 'Ye shall know even as ye are known.'"

Throughout the whole series of these papers there is manifest that noble patriotic spirit which shows itself in the last paragraph. There exists also an intelligent and unselfish spirit, so that as one finishes his reading there comes to mind a query as to the author who wrote thus in 1808--who was this early advocate of applied chemistry--this enthusiast in chemistry? Each article bears at its conclusion the initials ***J.C.***, which in several of the earlier articles are erroneously given as I.C. They throw no light on our curiosity and probably no one would ever have known whom ***J.C.*** represented had not the man himself in later life confessed that as a lad of twenty years he penned these papers. They are exceedingly well composed. They show a wide, general knowledge and also great familiarity with the science of chemistry. Their young author was James Cutbush.

When Robert Hare was twenty years of age he gave to the world one of the finest discoveries made by a chemist. Cutbush presented known chemical facts for the use and improvement of natural conditions. Might not the young men of these days, surrounded by every sort of help, make similar earnest and worthwhile contributions? They surely can do this if they are imbued with the spirit of the forefathers--the American spirit in chemistry.

Additional evidence of Cutbush's chemical activity at this early age may be seen in a contribution to the Philadelphia *Medical Museum* (1808) upon mercury fulminate. This interesting body he declared to be mercury oxalate and cited as his authority Aikin's Chemical and Mineralogical Dictionary. He believed that its oxalic acid content was due to the action of nitric acid upon alcohol. Such being the case, he argued that he saw no reason why the salt could not be prepared in a way by which "no alcohol is employed." Accordingly, he mixed intimately two parts of salt of sorrel and one part of red precipitate. Upon this mixture he poured sixteen parts of water, and rubbed the solid mass intimately together. In time the red-colored mass assumed an ash color, when it was collected on a filter and dried. In his own words--

> "On trying a part of this powder on an anvil with a hammer, it exploded very violently, the comparison of which to that prepared by Howard's process was nearly equal."

While Cutbush was in error, relative to the true composition of the fulminate, he at least gave to the scientific world a characteristic property of mercuric oxalate, which does explode with considerable violence, while at 180 deg. C. it quickly breaks down with a mild explosive effect. Singularly enough, he seems not to have abandoned the view that the interaction of alcohol and nitric acid give rise to oxalic acid.

While doing experimental work, Cutbush was active in the dissemination of science facts through the medium of his pen. Thus it was in this year (1808) that he published the "Useful Cabinet."

The surroundings of Cutbush were congenial. Woodhouse was at the zenith of his career. John Redman Coxe figured largely in Philadelphia science circles. The delightful and widely trained Benjamin Smith

Barton was a prime favorite with the younger men of science; Adam Seybert was laying the foundations of mineralogical chemistry and Gerard Troost was soon to appear and give additional zest and impetus to chemical research. To all these men Cutbush was known and favorably known, judging from his own allusions to them in his scattered writings. Of them all he seems to have entertained the strongest attachment to the celebrated Barton and the talented Coxe, although he wrote of Dr. Woodhouse as "an experimenter unequalled." It is strange, however, that his references to Robert Hare are few and meagre. It is not easy to understand why this should be the case. True, there existed local prejudices and cliques in the closing decades of the 18th Century and the opening decades of the 19th Century. They are to be deplored, but humanity is frail and perhaps it is wisest to pass them by, yet so many things could be better understood if all the facts were laid bare. Frequent favorable mention was made by Cutbush of John Redman Coxe, hence probably the appearance of several of his contributions in the pages of the Philadelphia *Medical Museum*, edited at this particular time by Coxe. For example, in 1809, Cutbush published an article on the formation of ether in this journal, and suggested that the product of the interaction of sulphuric acid and alcohol could be best purified by distilling it over manganese or lead dioxide and not over caustic potash as was customary. He also dwelt on the production of ethylene in this process, attributing its presence to the dehydrating action of sulphuric acid upon the alcohol. Momentarily, he rejoiced over this observation, believing it was new, but promptly subsided when he discovered that Fourcroy and Vauquelin had long before made the same observations and given the same explanation. Two years later (1811), in the same journal, Cutbush reported results gathered from experiments to determine the value of the hop to brewers. He said much in regard to its essential oil in the preparation of malt liquor and repeated earlier personal observations upon the importance of chemistry in the brewing operations--

> "An art in which, to the principles of chemistry, many improvements have been made. To our worthy and ingenious countryman, Mr. Hare, much praise is due for various improvements in this art, which, we may add, were in consequence of his correct principles in chemistry and natural philosophy."

Here is one of the few references to Robert Hare made by Cutbush. It was when Hare was devoting most of his time and mental energies to the development and improvement of his father's business. He applied his scientific knowledge to it, only in the end to have it fail through the conditions which came upon the country during the period of the War of 1812. One cannot easily forget the filial devotion of Robert Hare to his father in this particular business. Gladly would he have pursued pure science, but he knew his duty and assumed it, although unable to devote much time to science until 1818. But that story has been told. Another appreciation from Cutbush which appears years later reads as follows:

> "The deflagrator of Professor Hare of Philadelphia is an apparatus well calculated for many interesting experiments on galvanism. To that gentleman we are indebted for the compound blowpipe, which produces a very intense heat by the combustion of hydrogen in contact with oxygen gas. Notwithstanding Professor Clark of England has laid claim to the apparatus, and the use of hydrogen gas in this way, the merit of the discovery is due to our learned and ingenious countryman."

The next few years in the life of Cutbush were most interesting. He enjoyed mingling with his fellows, and it is recorded that in 1810 he became a member of Lodge No. 2, Free and Accepted Masons, comprising in its membership General Peter Muhlenberg and many other distinguished Philadelphians in various walks of life. Upon them he made an exceedingly favorable impression, because in June of 1811, Cutbush was made presiding officer of his Lodge and frequently thereafter he was invited to address his brethren upon some of the topics of the moment. It is quite certain that he also availed himself in his dignified position to inculcate a knowledge of science, and his favorite science chemistry in particular, for on the pages of the Freemason's Magazine for 1811 may be seen "Subjects and Importance of Chemistry"--an article for laymen in which is plainly set forth how the science enters every walk of life. In many respects it recalls the introductory chapter of Parke's Chemical Catechism, for it advises how chemistry

> "removes the veil from the fabric of Nature, and makes us acquainted with all the phenomena which happen around us."

The offerings of Cutbush were fitting and most timely. They aroused the interest of his audience and induced many to enter upon scientific pursuits. At one place he enlarged upon the wonderful medicinal properties of a chalybeate water near Colestown, N. J., giving its analysis and the healthful effect it seemed to produce on those who used it.

Again, in the December issue of the *Freemason's Magazine* (1881), he presented a most interesting, readable and succinct historical sketch of our science which concludes as follows:

> "Thus chemistry is become an entirely new science. It is no longer confined to the laboratory of the arts: it has extended its flights to the sublimest heights of philosophy, and pursues paths formerly regarded as impenetrable mysteries. Placed forever in the elevated rank it now holds, rich with all its new conquests, it is become the science

> most adapted to the sublime speculations of philosophy, the most useful in advancing all the operations of the arts, and the most rational for scientific amusement. Exact in its process, sure in its results, varied in its operations, without limits in its applications and its views, severe and geometrical in its reasoning, there is scarcely any human occupation which it does not enlighten, and upon the perfection of which it may not have great influence. It bestows great enjoyment to every class of individuals: and who would not be ambitious of becoming acquainted with a science which enlightens almost every species of human knowledge?"

Imagine for a moment the effect of such an enthusiastic proclamation of the powers of chemistry on the readers of the Magazine! It would be and no doubt was contagious, with the consequence that our science was called upon to aid infant industries. Cutbush was far-visioned and dreamed of the development of our Country's national resources. He had the spirit of Woodhouse, Seybert and others, who, too, were actuated for our Country's welfare, for its development physically and spiritually, and how better could this be accomplished than through the medium of science, and in large measure by chemical science?

In his historical resume Cutbush mentions some

> "of the philosophers who have ... cultivated and enriched the new theory of chemistry with discoveries which will forever give immortality to their names, we have to notice Aikin, Babington, Bancroft, Beddoes, Blagdon, Cavendish, Chenevix, Crichton, Cruickshank, Davy, Lord Dundonald, Lord Dundas, Fordyce, Garnett, Hatchett, Henry, Higgins, Hope, Howard, Kirvan, Bishop of Llandaff, Murray, Nicholson, Pearson, Tennant, Tilloch, Thompson, Wedgwood, and Wollaston; and

Achard, Crell, Gilbert, Gren, Goetling, Humboldt, Hermbstadt, Klaproth, Lowitz, Richter, Scherer, Tromsdorff, Westrumb, Wiegleb, Bertholet, Chaptal, Fourcroy, Lagrange, Guiton, Van Mons, Proust, Sequin, Vauquelin, etc., etc."

To the modern chemist these names probably represent little. Perhaps a few sound familiar, but the majority are unknown to him. For instance, who would be apt to say much about the Bishop of Llandaff, who wrote to Henry, author of one of the earliest and most delightful texts:

"CAMBRIDGE, Oct. 28, 1787."

"Sir--

"Allow me to return you my thanks of the obliging manner in which you conveyed to me the kind notice, which the Literary and Philosophical Society were pleased to take of my essay; and to assure you at the same time that it will give me great pleasure to be acquainted with a gentleman who is so eminently distinguished for his skill in chemistry, as you have shewn yourself to be. I have been told by good authority, of an odd fact relative to calcined mercury, the fact is this: A bottle which contained some calcined mercury which had been purchased in London was left standing without its cork for near thirty years without being looked at. When it was examined, the greater part of it was revivified.

"I have the honour to be, Sir,
    "Yr obliged servt
        "BP. LLANDAFF."

And this celebrated Bishop was no less a personage than Dr. Watson, whose "Chemical Essays" are most charming, instructive reading at the present moment. Students of the history of our science will find them to be so.

But all these early chemists--ancient, if you please--are gone. They cultivated chemistry with pleasure and ardor. Some left visible imprints, while scarce a vestige remains of others. Their labours have made our path easier. A century hence, many honoured to-day and respected for their achievements, will receive scant consideration, though the work of the present looms up large in our judgment.

The founding of the Columbian Chemical Society in 1811 was an event in the chemical circles of Philadelphia. The old Chemical Society of Philadelphia went out of existence in 1809, with the death of Woodhouse. The new organization was founded "by a number of persons desirous of cultivating chemical science." It comprised many young men zealous in research. The names of eminent foreigners and distinguished Americans are upon its rolls. Its meetings were monthly. Each year, at the fall opening, "an oration on some chemical subject" was delivered. Every month some member was appointed to read "an original chemical essay." It was recorded that

> "any person desirous of membership ... previous to his election ... shall read an original essay on some chemical subject on which any member may speak not more than ten minutes."

This feature was held to be important; at least the daily papers made note of it, as is evident from the subjoined excerpt:

> "The following gentlemen have been elected Junior members of the Columbian Chemical Society, during the last year, after having read original dissertations, the subjects of which are attached to their respective names:

"Mr. T. W. Robertson, 'Objections to the Existence of a Principle of Repulsion.'

"Mr. Francis Brognard, 'On Chemical Affinity.'

"Mr. Lewis Gerhardt, 'On Light.'

"Mr. Dudley Burwell, 'On the Chemical Properties and Medical Uses of Arsenic.'

"Mr. Jeremiah J. Foster, 'On the History, Nature and Properties of Oxygen Gas.'

"Mr. J. C. Foster, 'Objections to the Antiphlogistic Theory of Combustion.'

"Mr. Charles Gignilliat, 'On Hydrogen Gas.'

"Mr. John Bent, 'On Oxygen Gas.'"

The monthly meetings were announced in the city papers. The announcements appeared at intervals through a period of years, hence it may be assumed the Society was an active organization and that its members regarded it as of consequence. The personnel of its official family is not devoid of interest at present. A single volume of memoirs, printed in 1813, is still extant and may occasionally be seen; from it will be learned that the "Hon. Thomas Jefferson, Esq., was the Patron" of the Society and its President was "James Cutbush, Esq., Professor of Natural Philosophy, Chemistry and Mineralogy in St. John's College."

Turning to the table of contents two contributions from the President are observed. The first relates to the "Prognostic Signs of the

Weather" and the second is "On the Oxyacetite of Iron as a Test or Reagent for the Discovery of Arsenic." There is little chemistry in the first contribution, and the second possesses value chiefly in the qualitative way. They were evidently dashed off with the idea of arousing discussion, in the hope that serious efforts might be set in operation in certain directions.

The thought which intrudes itself in looking through the *Memoirs*, noting the character of the individuals in the membership, and upon recalling the chemical activities of Cutbush, is as to the man himself. Why should he, barely twenty-three years of age, be chosen to such an important and prominent station as that of President of the Columbian Chemical Society? What manner of man was he? What his qualifications, his fitness and his position in the science world of Philadelphia? A search through ancient volumes in many libraries failed to bring to light any facts bearing on these points. The only fact discovered that had any value came from a newspaper advertisement bearing the date October, 1819. It read:

> "Bleaching Liquor, *Artificial Musk*, *Phosphate of Mercury and other chemical Preparations*, prepared and sold by

"JAMES CUTBUSH
"Chemist and Apothecary
"No. 25 South Fourth Street, Phila.

> "where complete collections of chemical reagents are kept as usual."

Here is a hint as to the occupation of Cutbush. He was a chemist--presumably a manufacturing chemist, supplying the necessary reagents to persons desiring them for their chemical studies; and further he was a pharmacist serving the various requirements of the medical men of the City.

Thorough search through newspaper files disclosed that from the year 1811 and perhaps two years earlier, and extending up to the year 1813--various announcements were made by Cutbush as to lectures of a public nature. These help us realize the character of the individual and his work. For example--

"Dr. Cutbush's course of ***Evening Lectures on Chemistry*** will commence early in the second week in November, at the Laboratory in Videl's Court, in Second, near the Corner of Chestnut St."

and several months later the following notice was found--

"LECTURES
on
THEORETICAL AND PRACTICAL PHARMACY

"The subscriber, at the solicitation of several medical gentlemen, proposes to give a series of Lectures on the Theory and Practice of Pharmacy, accompanied with the necessary chemical elucidations.

"Tickets may be had at 25 South Fourth St.

"Price 20 dollars.

"JAMES CUTBUSH."

This was in the year 1812. Early in 1813, a year after the preceding announcement, there appeared--

"J. Cutbush has the pleasure to announce to the ladies and gentlemen composing his class that the lectures on Chemistry, as well as those which are to follow on Mineralogy and Natural Philosophy, will be given in St. John's Lyceum in a building lately erected at the Corner of Chester and Race, between Eighth and Ninth Sts.

"N.B. The next lecture will be delivered this evening (Saturday) when, at the request of several ladies, the nitrous oxide or the exhilarating gas will be exhibited."

These announcements exhibit a phase in the development of chemical science which is worthy of pause and reflection. Science subjects had taken hold of many persons in the early years of the Nineteenth Century. Some of them became ardent enthusiasts and missioners in the extension of those subjects. As early as 1808 M. Godon gave lectures on Mineralogy, and in 1810 announced a work of two volumes with a quarto supplement of charts. The science of chemistry also had its advocates. Cutbush was evidently one of them, although not the first. This honor belongs to Dr. Patrick Kerr Rogers, father of William B. Rogers, founder and first president of Massachusetts Institute of Technology and President of the National Academy of Science, of Dr. Henry D. Rogers, the eminent geologist, and of James B. and Robert E.--both distinguished in the chemical field.

It was in 1802 that Patrick K. Rogers received his medical degree and embarked upon practice. Having spare time, he began public lectures on the sciences, confining himself from 1807 to chemistry. He was very successful. One of his advertisements as it appeared in the *Aurora*, in 1809, read:

"EVENING LECTURES
MEDICAL AND CHEMICAL
For Gentlemen

DR. P. K. ROGERS

"Having commenced a course of experimental lectures on Chemistry to ladies, proposes to give a similar course to gentlemen at a different hour. Twelve o'clock is the hour fixed for the former, but as the gentlemen of the city are variously engaged in business during the day, an evening hour will be more convenient for them. The evening course is particularly intended to accommodate men who have a taste for scientific information and who cannot, on account of their respective engagements during the day, attend the lectures in the University.

"A course for gentlemen will commence on Tuesday and will terminate in the last week of February. The hour will be seven o'clock in the evening. Two lectures at least, sometimes three, will be delivered every week. About 1500 interesting experiments will be exhibited and submitted to the familiar inspection of the class. Several important experiments not hitherto introduced in any series of chemical demonstrations in this place will be displayed in the illustrations of different subjects.

"The laboratory is in the lecturer's house in South Ninth Street, opposite the University and is furnished with an excellent chemical apparatus.

"The tickets for this course will be ten dollars. The persons to take tickets will be entitled to the use of the lecturer's excellent medical and chemical library during the season.

"Persons wishing to attend this course will please call at the lecturer's home at any time before next Tuesday in order to enter the names on the list.

"Ladies are informed that the list of subscribers to their course will not be closed until next Monday at twelve o'clock at the hour the next lecture, properly the first of the regular series, will be delivered. Gentlemen are not admitted to these lectures."

In 1810 Dr. Rogers gave out a Syllabus of 12 octavo pages "On Experimental Lectures on Natural Philosophy and Chemistry," in which great emphasis was laid on the practical application of these sciences. It also stated that "it is even esteemed, in some measure, a cause of shame, for persons of respectable education, to be ignorant of their general principles." In one newspaper announcement Rogers said that in order to get sufficient space for his audience he had procured the "use of the elegant and spacious ball room of M. Guillou." In this special work he was repeating the labors of Sir Humphrey Davy in London. In reality, Rogers and his contemporaries and coadjutors were pioneer University Extension Lecturers. They sought to popularize the natural and physical sciences and also broaden the vision or outlook of their hearers. In the case of Cutbush there was a strong desire to utilize chemistry in manufacture. This he emphasized more strongly than any other lecturer.

Another participant in the science propaganda was Dr. Thomas P. Jones, who devoted himself to Chemistry. The following notice of his lecture course is not devoid of interest:

"On Saturday, the 13th inst., at seven o'clock in the evening, at Dr. Jones' Chemical Lecture Room, S.W. Corner of Fourth and Chestnut Streets, a lecture will be delivered on the properties of nitrous oxide, or the exhilarating gas, accompanied with a number of experiments. A large quantity will be prepared to exhibit its effects when inhaled.

"Tickets at fifty cents each may be had at A. Finley's Bookstore, S.E. Cor. of Chestnut and Fourth Streets, or at the lecture room on the stated evening."

On perusing early chemical texts and advertisements, such as those just given, attention is pointedly called to nitrous oxide, especially to its exhilarating properties, for then it was "laughing gas!" One Philip H. Nicklin published a brochure entitled

"THE ONLY GENTEEL WAY OF GETTING DRUNK

"A character representation of the effects produced by inhaling nitrous oxide gas. The accuracy of which no man breathing can deny. Price 25 cts."

To-day, nitrous oxide means a benign anaesthetic, so helpful and merciful when one is brought under the knife of the skillful surgeon.

The honor accorded Cutbush by his election to the Presidency of the Columbian Chemical Society was merited. He was not only an active, intelligent chemist, devoted to the advancement of his science in all directions, but he seems to have been an ardent enthusiast in the cause of education, for on the 7th of November, 1811, he delivered an Oration on Education before the Society for the Promotion of a Rational System of Education. His audience was large and consisted of the very best people of the city. The printed oration shows that in addition to his chemical knowledge he was versed in the humanities, in mathematics, in philosophy and ancient history. To-day the intelligent reader would pronounce the oration scholarly in every particular. His chief purpose seems to have been to introduce into what was then the customary curriculum in schools a definite amount of science--natural and physical. This is marked in the title of the organization before which he appeared on the occasion referred to, in Old St. John's Church. The whole community was interested in education. A society of educators had existed for a number of years. Neef had for a long time been advocating a system which was in reality a modification of the Pestallozian System, and men in every walk of life were seriously considering the innovations and advancements in this all-important subject.

Little can be found in regard to the Society for the Promotion of a Rational System of Education, but it may be inferred that the society had branches throughout the city and perhaps far beyond, because elsewhere Cutbush spoke of the society as under the Presidency of John Goodman, Esq., and that its purpose was to bring about a reformation in education. Further, Goodman was a prominent layman in the Church of Old St. John, who with his associates, Messrs. Greiner and Braeutigam, fellow churchmen, deeply impressed with the new thought, seem to have established a school "formed out of the Lutheran congregation of the Church of St. John ... instituted several professorships ... one of which, that of Chemistry, Mineralogy and Natural Philosophy" was conferred upon Cutbush, who proceeded to deliver courses on these subjects.

Desirous of learning something in regard to St. John's College, the authorities of St. John's Lutheran Church were consulted. It must be remembered that this is the oldest English-speaking Lutheran Church in America. It was founded by General Peter Gabriel Muhlenberg, and a unique distinction of this church is that in a period of 113 years it has had but three pastors. Nothing in the minutes of the church showed that a movement toward the establishment of a college had ever been made. Moreover, search in the archives of the State Department failed to bring to light the granting of a charter for an institution bearing the name of St. John's College, although in an old directory of Philadelphia, reference is made to St. John's College, and to the fact that Cutbush was Professor of Chemistry, Mineralogy and Natural Philosophy in it. The same source of information declared that "the lectures were held back of St. John's Church in Race Street." It may be questioned whether Messrs. Goodman, Greiner and Braeutigam, who were the leaders of the congregation in the early years of 1800, and enthusiasts in regard to the reformation in education, did not, perhaps, carry out their thought without consulting the rest of their church associates. In the history of the church there is a singular reference to the purchase of houses and lots which were known as "the fourteen chimneys" and the statement is made that the object of the purchase is not given. These "fourteen chimneys" may have been the buildings back of St. John's Church on Race Street.

Benjamin Smith Barton was another professor in St. John's College, who devoted himself to Natural History and Botany. Mr. Greiner, who was associated with Messrs. Goodman and Braeutigam also taught in the institution, and the head of the college or school was a Mr. Bachman, who later became a Lutheran clergyman and naturalist of high repute in South Carolina.

It is interesting at this far-away day to note the purposes of the Society for the promotion of education as set forth in its constitution. Among other things, it is said "the education of youth in useful knowledge ought to be a primary object with parents and friends, that more especially ought every endeavour to be made in a religious community to lay a sure and solid foundation for every moral and social virtue. Impressed with a conviction of this important truth, a number of the members of St. John's congregation, willing to give every aid within their power toward the establishment and support of a Rational System of Education, have formed themselves into a Society for that purpose."

The copy of Oration on Education, printed by Cutbush, which it was the privilege of the writer to peruse, was the copy handed by Cutbush "To Dr. Seybert with the compliments of the author." In spite of age, these words are very clear and legible, and if the only relic by which to judge of the character of Cutbush, would indicate him to be a man of intelligence.

There were many other societies extant at this period and through subsequent years which had for their object the promotion of scientific education. Among these was the Linnean Society, of which James Cutbush was Vice-President.

Cutbush had the honor of being one of the few of the original Society of Philadelphia for the Promotion of National Industry, whose essays excited the attention of the citizens of the United States. Samuel Jackson, M.D., Professor in the College of Apothecaries, was one of the most active members.

Amidst all the activities of Cutbush as a manufacturing chemist, as a teacher of the science, as a promoter of educational reforms, as a member of many organizations, he was very busy in a literary direction. For example, in 1812 he published a brochure on Hydrostatics, in which were described various hydrometers and their application. Numerous tables appear in it as well as many interesting and serviceable problems. It was designed for and was helpful to artisans and to beginners in the science of physics and chemistry. It is appropriately dedicated to the Columbian Chemical Society.

In the year 1813, Cutbush placed before the public his "Philosophy of Experimental Chemistry" in two volumes. It was dedicated to the "Professors and Students of the University of Pennsylvania and to the Trustees of St. John's College." One cannot fail to wonder why Cutbush should have so honoured the University when there is no record anywhere that he ever pursued studies under the aegis of the University. Indeed, it will probably remain a query as to where he was educated. He is often spoken of as "Doctor Cutbush" and in at least two instances the title "M.D." is placed after his name, yet it is a fact that in no place where he personally was responsible for the printing of his name is there any title affixed to it. Every source of information from which it was hoped to ascertain where Cutbush might have obtained the Doctorate in the first decade of the 19th Century failed to produce the fact. Libraries were searched and volumes that ordinarily convey such information were studied without positive result.

The little contribution on the "Philosophy of Chemistry" was favorably known, for Silliman, in his reference to Gorham's Chemistry as the first book upon this subject by a native American, credits Cutbush with having written a similar work, but speaks of the effort of Cutbush as more elementary and not as exhaustive as that of Gorham. The introduction in the first volume of Cutbush's work will always be interesting to American students of the science. For example, this quotation:

> "Several original works have, accordingly, appeared, and some editions of European treatises have been published with revisions, corrections and additions by our countrymen. The Chemical and Economical Essays of Pennington, the edition of Chaptal enlarged by the late James Woodhouse ... that of Henry's Chemistry by Professor Silliman of Yale College, with some others, evince not only the learning and talents of our

countrymen, but a growing taste for the encouragement of learning and the acquisition of chemical knowledge. Besides these, in the Transactions of our Societies and in the journals, or periodical works, several valuable papers have appeared. The genius of the medical students of the University of Pennsylvania, in particular, has been shown in a number of excellent inaugural dissertations, some of which have added to the improvement of chemical science.

"The first teacher of chemistry was Dr. Benjamin Rush ... who may justly be styled the father of chemistry in America. He commenced a course of lectures on this science in the then College of Philadelphia; and although chemistry at that day (1768) may be said to have been in its infancy, yet the Doctor did honour to the chair, the school, and his country. We now speak of him only as a chemist.... The advancement of chemistry in our city ... is also indebted to other institutions. The American Philosophical Society, the College of Physicians, instituted in 1787, the Medical Society, formed in 1771; the Chemical Society under the patronage of Doctors Woodhouse and Seybert, which has since been dissolved; the Linnean Society, instituted under the presidency of the learned Dr. Benjamin Smith Barton; the Columbian Chemical Society, founded in 1811; the Academy of Natural Science--all show the zeal for useful knowledge and philosophical inquiry.... For the introduction of popular chemistry, the citizens of Philadelphia are also indebted to Doctors Rogers and Jones, and to Benjamin Tucker, who have taught Chemistry with much zeal and talents."

Many attractions are found in the Philosophy of Experimental Chemistry. The first discussion is that on Chemical Affinity. Two experiments are introduced. In the first it is stated

"If equal parts, by weight, of sulphur and mercury be introduced into a crucible, and in this situation exposed to a sufficient heat; a compound will be formed, called sulphuret of mercury."

In the second experiment the student is advised to

"Mix together sulphur and potash, and throw them into water; the sulphur will separate. If the same articles be put into a crucible and melted, and then thrown into water, the sulphur as well as the potash will be dissolved."

And next comes the

"Rationale. In the first experiment there is an instance of chemical action, as well as of single affinity, for the sulphur and mercury would remain separate if heat was not applied. In consequence of this agent, they unite into an uniform whole, totally inseparable by mechanical means, and possessing characters distinct from either of its constituent parts.

"In the second experiment, the union of sulphur with potash is effected by heat; for if a sulphuret was not formed, no solution of the sulphur would take place. Hence it is that chemical action is the consequence of a power, without which it could never ensue, and with which it always acts in unison. This power is affinity."

Then it is remarked:

"Chemistry is a science, which has for its object to discover the constituent properties of bodies, the result of the various combinations, and the laws by which those combinations are effected. Its operations being either analytical or synthetical, consist of composition, or decomposition. The laws which govern chemical changes have been resolved into those of attraction or affinity. Affinity of composition of chemical affinity differs from that of aggregation or cohesion or corpuscular attraction, by acting upon matter of a different kind; or by taking place between the ultimate constituent parts of bodies, producing by its action, substances possessing properties frequently very different, and sometimes contrary to those of the constituent parts."

Throughout the book the order of presentation is the experiment, rationale, and remarks. A study of the "Philosophy" shows clearly that Cutbush presented his material in a rather original fashion. His method is not observable in any of the text-books of that date.

In discussing potash, Cutbush wrote:

"It has been supposed ever since our countryman, Dr. Woodhouse, made an experiment with potash that this alkali had an inflammable base. I am disposed to believe that the Doctor was the first one who hazarded this conjecture as to the inflammable nature of potash ***when treated in certain ways***. The Doctor found that a mixture of pearl ash with soot, calcined by a very intense heat in a covered crucible, when cold caught fire on the affusion of water. The experiment was repeated with charcoal with the same result and the inflammation probably arose from the action of the base of the alkali on the water."

He says:

> "That Thomas Cooper ... repeated this experiment, and succeeded, I think, after several attempts, in procuring the metal. Dr. John Redman Coxe and myself also performed it, but in our attempt we failed. The professor, however, persevered, and finally procured it.... My brother, Dr. Edward Cutbush, succeeded in procuring it by using the heat of a black-smith's forge. I have not heard of any other attempts in this country except by a gentleman in New York, who was also successful."

These statements substantiate the idea that Woodhouse isolated the metal potassium quite independently from any European chemist; it even looks as if he may have isolated it in the manner referred to before Sir Humphrey Davy had separated it with the aid of the electric current.

In the first volume of the Philosophy there is a frontispiece, a lamp furnace, consisting of a brass rod, fastened to a piece of metal, furnished with rings of different diameters, and thumb screws to raise or lower the lamp and rings when in use. By this furnace evaporation, digestion, solution, sublimation, distillation and other processes, which require a low temperature, may be performed.

And in the second volume there is a frontispiece representing a portable universal furnace, made of strong wrought iron plates and lined with bricks bedded in fire-proof loam. The height of the furnace is two feet. The body of the furnace is elliptical. There are three openings in front of the furnace, one above the other, furnished with sliding doors, and fitted with stoppers made of crucible ware.

Both pieces of apparatus represent a marked advancement. They were evidently exceedingly useful. By their means it was possible to execute excellent work.

It would repay one to examine with care the various American text-books on chemistry, beginning about 1770 and continuing down to 1830. There would arise a picture before one's mind of the successive steps in the development of chemical apparatus, and again, the knowledge derived from the presentation of chemical theory and data would be refreshing and inspirational. It is to be hoped that the time is not far distant when some library, public or university library, will go to the trouble of gathering the American texts on Chemistry for the period just alluded to. It is not likely that an alcove filled with this literature would be largely patronized, yet it would be possible for the enthusiast on the development of chemistry in this country to collect from such a source a great deal of valuable material which might be presented with profit to the rising generation of American chemists.

Cutbush had little leisure during the year 1813, as he was engaged with the duties of the College and was conducting popular lectures on an extended scale. It was necessary for him to invite his friend, Dr. George F. Lehman, to assist in the various demonstrations. They emphasized not only the theory but the practice of chemistry with its application to the useful arts. Their experiments were numerous and were of such a character as to appeal to the general public. The course offered by Professor Cutbush and Dr. Lehman was remunerative. It is said the cost of tickets for ladies was $5.00 and those for gentlemen $8.00.

In addition to the devotion of Cutbush to these didactic courses in chemistry, he spent much time in a literary way. One of the best-known publishers of the city announced the purpose of printing the *American*

Artist's Manual under the editorship of Cutbush. The advertisement stated--

> "To manufacturers, however, who are presumed to be interested in practical knowledge the value of such works is greatly diminished by the multiplicity of theories, technical terms and complicated processes which they in general contain. It is, therefore, unnecessary to expatiate on the advantages to be derived from such a publication as is now proposed in the present work. While it is intended to embrace most of the Arts and Manufactures, particular attention will be paid to those of agriculture, brewing, bleaching, dyeing in its various branches, the manufacture of glass, pottery and all others which the situation of our country renders obviously of primary concern and importance."

This extensive and helpful publication appeared in 1814 in two octavo volumes of more than 600 pages each. The reader should note that

> "The price to subscribers will be $7.00 in boards or $8.00 substantially bound, payable on delivery. Those who procure subscriptions of nine copies and become accountable for their payment shall be entitled to one copy for their trouble."

The book was dedicated to Benjamin Smith Barton. No title of any kind appears after the author's name, indicating that he had probably by the year 1814 severed his connection with all his educational projects in Philadelphia. In the preface the author speaks of

> "Having devoted the greater part of his life to chemical pursuits."

Glancing through these volumes the impression made upon the reader was that the author had read widely in the sciences, but particularly in his favorite science, chemistry. The book is really a popular dictionary of chemical technology. While it is sparsely illustrated, early forms of chemical glassware are pictured. From these may be gathered the story of the gradual development of very useful apparatus, for example, such as is used in various kinds of distillation.

That Cutbush had probably ceased his professional duties by the year 1814, as has just been hinted, is further emphasized on noting that he was appointed Assistant Apothecary General in the U. S. Army on the twelfth day of August in the year 1814. What his duties as such may have been has not been discovered. It would not be fair to call it a radical change in position, but it was a change which necessitated Cutbush giving more thought and attention to pharmacy, which in his earlier career was a secondary subject, but in which he was so proficient that he attracted to himself the attention of leading men in medical circles. He was in Philadelphia, prosecuting his duties as late as the year 1819. It is known that during this period he was attached to the Northern Division of the Army.

In 1820 Dr. James Lovell, Surgeon General of the Army, suggested to General Thayer, Superintendent of the Military Academy at West Point, that Cutbush be appointed Chief Medical Officer at the Academy and Post of West Point. In this capacity he served for seventeen months, when he became Acting Professor of Chemistry and Mineralogy in the Academy. The first lecture in his new position was delivered October 9, 1820. In a sense, it marked the beginning of a new career for Cutbush. He resumed teaching duties, but gave himself more particularly to the study, not only of gunpowder, which never ceased to be interesting to him, but to explosives of higher character, and in this latter field he reached his greatest eminence and may confidently be regarded as a pioneer in it.

Just before leaving Philadelphia, in the year 1820, Cutbush wrote Benjamin Silliman at some length on an improvement of the Voltaic electrical lamp. It was an ingenious modification and constituted the first contribution made by Cutbush to the *American Journal of Science*.

But, returning to his life at West Point, it may be observed that in 1822 he contributed his second article to the *Journal of Science*, which did not appear in print, however, until 1824. This article related to the composition and properties of the Chinese fire and the so-called brilliant fires. It was very interesting. It displayed a thorough and wide knowledge of pyrotechnics with which Cutbush, in previous years, had been gradually familiarizing himself. At one point he said:

> "Most if not all the compositions used in fireworks, including military fireworks, were more the result of the labours of the artisan who was neither controlled by fixed principles nor by a knowledge of the effects and properties of bodies and of the systematic experiments of the chemist, and yet in consequence of some fortuitous and repeated trials we find that he has been successful, and moreover has amassed a body of facts which we may reasonably infer may either be rendered more perfect by knowledge or improved upon by the exact aid of chemical science."

Here is every proof of his purpose to apply his understanding of chemical principles and his own experience to the solution of pyrotechnic problems, for he continues:

> "Pyrotechnics is at present considered under two heads, namely, fireworks for exhibition and military fireworks. The latter is undoubtedly the most useful, as it embraces a variety of propositions calculated for attack and defence both for naval and land service."

Almost simultaneously there appeared in the same *Journal of Arts and Science* another contribution by Cutbush, entitled

REMARKS CONCERNING THE COMPOSITION AND PROPERTIES OF THE
GREEK FIRE

In the light of recent events and the use of all sorts of chemical bodies for warfare and destruction it will not be uninteresting to introduce here a few paragraphs from this remarkable contribution. He says:

> "The Greek fire was invented by Callinicus of Heliopolis, a town in Syria, who used it with so much skill and effect during a naval engagement that he destroyed a whole fleet of the enemy, in which were embarked 30,000 men.

> "It appears that in the reign of Louis XV, a chemist of Grenoble, Dupre de Mayen, discovered a composition similar in effect to the Greek fire of Callinicus, which was exhibited at Brest, and proved successful, but the preparation was kept secret. The original Greek fire was used in 1291, and also in 1679.... Writers have defined it to be a sort of artificial fire, which burns with increased violence when it mixes with water.... That it was a liquid composition, we may infer from the modes of using it, which were several. It was employed chiefly on board of ships, and thrown on the vessels of the

enemy by large engines. It was sometimes kindled in particular vessels, which might be called fire ships, and which were introduced among a hostile fleet. Sometimes it was put into jars and other vessels, and thrown at the enemy by means of projectile machines, and sometimes it was *squirted* by soldiers from hand engines, or blown through pipes. This fire was also discharged from the *foreparts of ships* by a machine constructed of copper and iron, the extremity of which is said to have resembled the *open mouth* and *jaws* of a lion or other animal. They were painted, and even gilded, and were capable of projecting the liquid fire to a great distance.

"... John Cameniata, speaking of his native city, Thessalonica, which was taken by the Saracens in the year 904, says that the enemy threw fire into the wooden works of the besieged, which was blown into them by means of tubes, and thrown from other vessels.... This proves that the Greeks, in the beginning of the Tenth Century, were no longer the only people acquainted with the art of preparing this fire, the *precursor of our gunpowder*. The Emperor Leo, who about the same period wrote his *Art of War*, recommends such engines, with a metal covering, to be constructed in the foreparts of ships, and he twice afterwards mentions engines for throwing out Greek fire.... For many centuries the method of making this dreadful article of destruction was lost; but it has just been discovered by the librarian of the elector of Bavaria, who has found a very old Latin manuscript which contains directions for preparing it.

"... On the subject of incendiary and other military fireworks, the French have certainly laid the foundation for the very preparations now used by the British, for the formulae for such preparations may be traced to the French service....

"The Moors were in possession of the secret for preparing the Greek fire in 1432, according to the testimony of Brocquire. Bertrandon de la Brocquire was in Palestine in 1432 as counsellor to the Duke of Burgundy. He was present at Barrat during one of the Moorish celebrations. 'It began,' he remarks, 'in the evening at sunset. Numerous companies scattered here and there were singing, and uttering loud cries. While this was passing, the cannon of the castle was fired, and the people of the town launched into the air "bein haut et bein loin, une maniere de fue plus gros fellot que je veisse oncques allume." They told me they made use of such at sea, to set fire to the sails of an enemy's vessel.
It seems to me that it is a thing easy to be made, and at a little expense it may be equally well employed to burn a camp or a thatched village, or in an engagement with cavalry to frighten their horses. Curious to know its composition, I sent the servant of my host to the person who made this fire, and requested him to teach me his method. He returned for answer, that he dare not, for that he should run great danger were it known; but there is nothing a man will not do for money. I offered him a ducat, which quieted his fears, and he taught me all he knew, and even gave me the moulds in wood, with the other ingredients, which I have brought to France.'
... When Constantinople was attacked, the Emperor Leo burnt the vessels or boats, to the number of one thousand eight hundred, by means of the Greek fire.... Its composition was kept secret at Constantinople, pretending that the knowledge of it came from an angel to the first and greatest of the Constantines, with a sacred injunction not to divulge it under any pretext, etc. It ... was kept secret above 400

years ... was stolen by the Mahometans, who employed it against the Crusaders. A knight, it appears, who despised the swords and lances of the Saracens, relates, with heartfelt sincerity, his own fears at the sight and sound of the mischievous engine that discharged a torrent of fire. 'It came flying through the air, like a winged, long-tailed dragon, about the thickness of a hogshead, with a report of thunder, and the velocity of lightning; and the darkness of the night was dispelled by this deadly illumination. The use of the Greek, or as it might now be called the Saracen fire, was continued to the middle of the Fourteenth Century, when the scientific or casual compound of nitre, sulphur and charcoal effected a new revolution in the art of war, and the history of mankind.' ... We do not know of any imitation of the original Greek fire having been used in modern warfare, but have no hesitation in believing that naphtha prepared as already stated would in many cases prove advantageous. It seems to be well calculated for close naval combat, if the object be to destroy the sails and rigging of an enemy's ship. The rapidity and extent of its combustion, added to the circumstances of its peculiar properties, that of resisting the action of water in particular, contribute altogether to this opinion."

The entire article from which these excerpts have been made is worthy of study, even at this late date. It is suggestive and carries with it many historical references of value. The enthusiasm of Cutbush for pyrotechnic bodies is manifest in every line of this publication.

About a year later (1823) Cutbush discussed the formation of cyanogen in processes not previously noticed. He spoke of the appearance of this gas in the putrefaction of animal and vegetable matter, making the following remarkable and in some respects startling statement:

> "I believe it would be found that the compound (carburet of azote) is the basis of the miasmata which produces malignant, bilious diseases.... Marsh miasmata are generally the cause of intermittent fevers. Now under particular circumstances of action may we not admit the generation of carburet of azote or cyanogen, and if so, as it readily unites with hydrogen, may it not be the miasma which produces malignant bilious fevers, since it is known that hydrocyanic acid is destructive to animal life and a most virulent poison?... Miasmata of some kind are the cause of yellow fever. For our part we believe it to be carburet of azote, or of some of its combinations, and of these that with hydrogen, from its deleterious character, seems to be the one."

Another observation made in this connection was that cyanogen is produced when charcoal is heated with nitric acid. Cutbush stated that he placed charcoal and nitric acid together in a retort and subjected them to distillation, collecting the product in Woulfe's bottles, after which the resulting solutions were impregnated with potash, and

> "common sulphate and persulphate of iron introduced. The colour instantly changed and became more or less blue, proving the existence of the perferrocyanite of iron and, consequently, of cyanogen."

Having never met this method of preparing cyanogen, experiments were made in the writer's laboratory to verify the statement. A blue, or what had the semblance of a blue color, could be obtained at the point given by Cutbush, but just as soon as the solution was acidulated, as is always done, the precipitate disappeared and there was not the slightest indication that Prussian blue had been formed. Even after hours of rest there was not a sign of it.

Association on the part of Cutbush with the men of science in Philadelphia during the first decade of the Nineteenth Century led to an extension of his interest in science circles, so that during leisure moments at West Point (1824) he wrote of the following minerals observed by him in and near that place:

> "Molybdenite, kaolin, tremolite, schorl, adularia, garnet, actinolite, precious serpentine (remarkably elegant), epidote and diallage."

Recently, attention has been called to a volume by Cutbush entitled "Lectures on the Adulteration of Food and Culinary Poisons.... With a Means of Discovering Them and Rules for Determining the Purity of Substances." It was published at Newburgh, N. Y., in 1823. The writer has never seen this volume. His search for it has been unsuccessful.

Another publication was "A Synopsis of Chemistry, Arranged Alphabetically, Comprehending the Names, Synonyms, and Definitions in that Science." New York: E. Lewis, 1821. This book is also exceedingly rare.

The real magnum opus of Cutbush resulted in "A System of Pyrotechny" (1825), which voluminous publication did not appear until after his decease, and then largely through the efforts of his wife and former students in the Cadet Corps, for, in *Silliman's Journal*, this note appeared:

> "Mrs. Cutbush, widow of the late Dr. Cutbush, of West Point, proposes to publish by subscription a Treatise on Pyrotechny by her husband, Dr. James Cutbush.... By the reputation which Dr. Cutbush sustained, as well as by the ability which his elaborate treatises on these subjects already published in this journal display, there can be no doubt that this

posthumous work will be worthy of the public patronage, which we hope will be liberally bestowed."

Even to-day this publication stands out preeminently and for years has been referred to by artisans and by scientists. Chapters dealing with military fireworks have been seriously studied. In the light of the violent fires, grenades, etc., used in the late war the writings of Cutbush become very fascinating. They show that he truly blazed the way in this field. In the introduction to this splendid volume he wrote:

"On this head, that of the application of chemistry to pyrotechny, we claim so much originality, as, so far as we know, to have been the first, who applied the principles of chemistry.... As this subject, however interesting to the theoretical pyrotechnist, cannot be understood without a knowledge of chemistry, it is obvious that that science is a powerful aid to pyrotechny.... Viewing pyrotechny either as a science or an art, there is undoubtedly required in its prosecution much skill and practice. The mere artificer or fireworker by constant habit may understand, it is true, how to mix minerals, prepare composition, charge cases, etc., ... but without a knowledge of chemistry he cannot understand the theory.... Indeed, chemistry is indispensable to pyrotechny."

Much time and thought were given by Cutbush in the experimental development of this particular subject in his own laboratory. In reading upon the subject he had collected a vast material which was then put to crucial experimental tests. These, outside of his teaching hours, occupied his whole attention.

An outline of how the work in the chemical department of the United States Military Academy was conducted will not be devoid of interest.

First Year

Theory and Experimental Chemistry.

Second Year

Application of Chemistry to the Arts, Manufactures and Domestic Economy, constituting along with Mineralogy the second course.

Pyrotechny naturally was developed quite extensively. Teachers of chemistry will note with pleasure the questions which Cutbush arranged for his student corps, particularly those questions which had to do with pyrotechny:

"What is saltpetre? What is nitric acid? What are the sources of saltpetre, and how it is obtained? How is it formed in nitre beds, extracted, and refined? What circumstances are necessary to produce nitre, and how does animal matter act in its production? What is the difference between the old and new process for refining saltpetre? What reagents are used to discover the presence of foreign substances in nitre? What are nitre caves? Where do they exist? What are the nitre caves of the western country, and how is nitre extracted from the earth? What proportion of nitre does the saltpetre of the nitrate caves afford? What is the theory of the process for extracting saltpetre from nitrous earth, or nitrate of lime? What is sulphur? How is it obtained, and how is it purified for the manufacture of gunpowder? Of what use is sulphur in the composition of gunpowder? Does it add to the effective force of gunpowder? What is charcoal? What is the best mode of carbonizing wood for the purpose of gunpowder? What woods are preferred for this purpose? In the charring of wood, what part is converted into coal, and what gas and acid are disengaged? What is the use of charcoal in gunpowder? What is gunpowder? What are considered the best proportions for forming it, and what constitutes the difference between powder for war, for gunning, and for mining? How does the combustion of gunpowder take place? Can you explain why combustion takes place without the presence of a gaseous supporter of combustion, as gunpowder will inflame in vacuo? What are the products of the combustion of gunpowder? What gases are generated? To what is the force of fired gunpowder owing? What are the experiments of Mr. Robins on the force of gunpowder? How would you separate the component parts of gunpowder so as to determine their proportions? What are gunpowder proofs? What is understood by the comparative force of gunpowder? What are eprouvettes, etc.? In noticing in the same manner the preparations used for fireworks, and for war, as the rocket, for instance, the following questions were propounded; viz., What is a rocket? How is it formed? Is the case always made of paper? What is the war rocket? What is the composition for rockets, and how does it act? What particular care is required in charging a rocket? What is the cause of the ascension of rockets? What is the use of the conical cavity, made in a rocket at the time it is charged, or bored out after it is charged? How do cases charged with composition impart motion to wheels, and other pieces of fireworks? What is understood by the rocket principle? What is the rocket stick and its use? Is the centre of gravity fixed, or is it shifting in the flight of rockets? How are rockets discharged? What is the head of a rocket? What is usually put in the head? Are all rockets furnished with a head? What is understood by the furniture of a rocket? How are the serpents, stars, fire-rain, etc., forming the furniture of a rocket, discharged into the air, when the rocket has terminated its flight, or arrived at its maximum of ascension? What forms the difference between a balloon, in fireworks, and a rocket? As the balloon contains also furniture, and is projected vertically from a mortar, how is fire communicated to it, so as to burst it in the air? Is the fuse used, in this case, the same as that for bombs, howitzers, and grenades? What is the Asiatic rocket? The fougette of the French? In what siege were they employed with success by the native troops of India? What was the nature of their war-rocket? What is the murdering rocket of the French? Is the conical head hollow, solid, blunt, or pointed? Why is it called the murdering rocket? What is the Congreve rocket? Is Congreve the inventor or improver of this rocket? What are Congreve rockets loaded or armed with? In what part is the load placed? Is the case made up of paper or sheet-iron? What are the sizes of Congreve rockets?"

In the introduction to "Pyrotechnics" Cutbush remarked that he had consulted many authorities without much advantage, finding the French the most helpful. Of the English he said:

"As respects the turtle torpedo and catamarin submarine machines, it appears that Bushnel claims the originality of the discovery from the date of his invention, although similar contrivances had long ago been suggested. Fulton's improvements, in the torpedo, are deserving of particular attention, but it is plain that the Catamarin of the English is the same in principle and application as Fulton's torpedo and that Fulton deserves the merit of it."

The "System of Pyrotechny" bears the ear-marks of much careful experimental study. It is a most worthy contribution, and is strong proof of the dominating force in the mind of Cutbush, namely, to make his science as widely useful as possible. Chemists may justly take pride in this early contribution in the application of chemical principles.

The life story of Cutbush has now been told. It is really the story of his life activities, for regrettable as it is, there does lack a picture of the man's personality. The parents of James Cutbush were Edward Cutbush and Anne Marriat. The father was a stone-cutter or carver. To these good people were given four children: Edward, born in 1772; Ann, in 1782 (who died in 1798); William, born in 1785, and James in 1788. Edward became prominent as a naval surgeon, while William graduated from West Point in 1812, and attained eminence as an engineer.

Indeed, at an early age, William was a midshipman in the United States Navy, and was taken prisoner by the Algerines at the time the frigate Philadelphia ran aground in the harbor of Tripoli, from which he was released after two years' confinement in prison, and returned to the United States, when he became a cadet in the Military Academy.

James Cutbush must have been a man of mark among his neighbors--as indicated by sundry positions of trust which he held. Further, he must have been a favorite with the Cadet Corps at West Point, where he was buried. His tomb there bears this inscription:

> "Sacred to the memory of Dr. James Cutbush, Member of the American Philosophical Society, Late Surgeon, U. S. Army and Professor of Chemistry at the U. S. Military Academy, West Point, N. Y., who departed this life December 15, 1823, aged 35 years. An honourable tribute of respect from his grateful pupils."

The work of Cutbush was of the genuine pioneer character, and enriched the annals of American chemistry. While it would be delightful to know more of the man, cruel fate compels us to be content with the estimate, brief though it is, given in Poulsen's *American Daily Advertiser*, December 23, 1823:

> "A man not only known for his extensive knowledge of chemistry, but distinguished for his philosophy and patriotism."

www.bookjungle.com *email:* sales@bookjungle.com *fax:* 630-214-0564 *mail:* Book Jungle PO Box 2226 Champaign, IL 61825

The Codes Of Hammurabi And Moses
W. W. Davies

QTY

The discovery of the Hammurabi Code is one of the greatest achievements of archaeology, and is of paramount interest, not only to the student of the Bible, but also to all those interested in ancient history...

Religion   **ISBN:** *1-59462-338-4*   Pages:132
MSRP $12.95

The Theory of Moral Sentiments
Adam Smith

QTY

This work from 1749. contains original theories of conscience amd moral judgment and it is the foundation for systemof morals.

Philosophy **ISBN:** *1-59462-777-0*   Pages:536
MSRP $19.95

Jessica's First Prayer
Hesba Stretton

QTY

In a screened and secluded corner of one of the many railway-bridges which span the streets of London there could be seen a few years ago, from five o'clock every morning until half past eight, a tidily set-out coffee-stall, consisting of a trestle and board, upon which stood two large tin cans, with a small fire of charcoal burning under each so as to keep the coffee boiling during the early hours of the morning when the work-people were thronging into the city on their way to their daily toil...

Childrens   **ISBN:** *1-59462-373-2*   Pages:84
MSRP $9.95

My Life and Work
Henry Ford

QTY

Henry Ford revolutionized the world with his implementation of mass production for the Model T automobile. Gain valuable business insight into his life and work with his own auto-biography... "We have only started on our development of our country we have not as yet, with all our talk of wonderful progress, done more than scratch the surface. The progress has been wonderful enough but..."

Biographies/ **ISBN:** *1-59462-198-5*   Pages:300
MSRP $21.95

www.bookjungle.com email: sales@bookjungle.com fax: 630-214-0564 mail: Book Jungle PO Box 2226 Champaign, IL 61825

The Art of Cross-Examination
Francis Wellman

QTY

I presume it is the experience of every author, after his first book is published upon an important subject, to be almost overwhelmed with a wealth of ideas and illustrations which could readily have been included in his book, and which to his own mind, at least, seem to make a second edition inevitable. Such certainly was the case with me; and when the first edition had reached its sixth impression in five months, I rejoiced to learn that it seemed to my publishers that the book had met with a sufficiently favorable reception to justify a second and considerably enlarged edition. ...

Reference   ISBN: *1-59462-647-2*

Pages:412
MSRP $19.95

On the Duty of Civil Disobedience
Henry David Thoreau

QTY

Thoreau wrote his famous essay, On the Duty of Civil Disobedience, as a protest against an unjust but popular war and the immoral but popular institution of slave-owning. He did more than write—he declined to pay his taxes, and was hauled off to gaol in consequence. Who can say how much this refusal of his hastened the end of the war and of slavery ?

Law   ISBN: *1-59462-747-9*

Pages:48
MSRP $7.45

Dream Psychology Psychoanalysis for Beginners
Sigmund Freud

QTY

Sigmund Freud, born Sigismund Schlomo Freud (May 6, 1856 - September 23, 1939), was a Jewish-Austrian neurologist and psychiatrist who co-founded the psychoanalytic school of psychology. Freud is best known for his theories of the unconscious mind, especially involving the mechanism of repression; his redefinition of sexual desire as mobile and directed towards a wide variety of objects; and his therapeutic techniques, especially his understanding of transference in the therapeutic relationship and the presumed value of dreams as sources of insight into unconscious desires.

Psychology   ISBN: *1-59462-905-6*

Pages:196
MSRP $15.45

The Miracle of Right Thought
Orison Swett Marden

QTY

Believe with all of your heart that you will do what you were made to do. When the mind has once formed the habit of holding cheerful, happy, prosperous pictures, it will not be easy to form the opposite habit. It does not matter how improbable or how far away this realization may see, or how dark the prospects may be, if we visualize them as best we can, as vividly as possible, hold tenaciously to them and vigorously struggle to attain them, they will gradually become actualized, realized in the life. But a desire, a longing without endeavor, a yearning abandoned or held indifferently will vanish without realization.

Self Help   ISBN: *1-59462-644-8*

Pages:360
MSRP $25.45

www.bookjungle.com *email: sales@bookjungle.com fax: 630-214-0564 mail: Book Jungle PO Box 2226 Champaign, IL 61825*

QTY

☐ **The Rosicrucian Cosmo-Conception Mystic Christianity** by *Max Heindel*   ISBN: *1-59462-188-8*   **$38.95**
The Rosicrucian Cosmo-conception is not dogmatic, neither does it appeal to any other authority than the reason of the student. It is: not controversial, but is: sent forth in the, hope that it may help to clear...   New Age/Religion Pages 646

☐ **Abandonment To Divine Providence** by *Jean-Pierre de Caussade*   ISBN: *1-59462-228-0*   **$25.95**
"The Rev. Jean Pierre de Caussade was one of the most remarkable spiritual writers of the Society of Jesus in France in the 18th Century. His death took place at Toulouse in 1751. His works have gone through many editions and have been republished...   Inspirational/Religion Pages 400

☐ **Mental Chemistry** by *Charles Haanel*   ISBN: *1-59462-192-6*   **$23.95**
Mental Chemistry allows the change of material conditions by combining and appropriately utilizing the power of the mind. Much like applied chemistry creates something new and unique out of careful combinations of chemicals the mastery of mental chemistry...   New Age Pages 354

☐ **The Letters of Robert Browning and Elizabeth Barret Barrett 1845-1846 vol II**   ISBN: *1-59462-193-4*   **$35.95**
by *Robert Browning* and *Elizabeth Barrett*   Biographies Pages 596

☐ **Gleanings In Genesis (volume I)** by *Arthur W. Pink*   ISBN: *1-59462-130-6*   **$27.45**
Appropriately has Genesis been termed "the seed plot of the Bible" for in it we have, in germ form, almost all of the great doctrines which are afterwards fully developed in the books of Scripture which follow...   Religion/Inspirational Pages 420

☐ **The Master Key** by *L. W. de Laurence*   ISBN: *1-59462-001-6*   **$30.95**
In no branch of human knowledge has there been a more lively increase of the spirit of research during the past few years than in the study of Psychology, Concentration and Mental Discipline. The requests for authentic lessons in Thought Control, Mental Discipline and...   New Age/Business Pages 422

☐ **The Lesser Key Of Solomon Goetia** by *L. W. de Laurence*   ISBN: *1-59462-092-X*   **$9.95**
This translation of the first book of the "Lernegton" which is now for the first time made accessible to students of Talismanic Magic was done, after careful collation and edition, from numerous Ancient Manuscripts in Hebrew, Latin, and French...   New Age/Occult Pages 92

☐ **Rubaiyat Of Omar Khayyam** by *Edward Fitzgerald*   ISBN: *1-59462-332-5*   **$13.95**
Edward Fitzgerald, whom the world has already learned, in spite of his own efforts to remain within the shadow of anonymity, to look upon as one of the rarest poets of the century, was born at Bredfield, in Suffolk, on the 31st of March, 1809. He was the third son of John Purcell...   Music Pages 172

☐ **Ancient Law** by *Henry Maine*   ISBN: *1-59462-128-4*   **$29.95**
The chief object of the following pages is to indicate some of the earliest ideas of mankind, as they are reflected in Ancient Law, and to point out the relation of those ideas to modern thought.   Religiom/History Pages 452

☐ **Far-Away Stories** by *William J. Locke*   ISBN: *1-59462-129-2*   **$19.45**
"Good wine needs no bush, but a collection of mixed vintages does. And this book is just such a collection. Some of the stories I do not want to remain buried for ever in the museum files of dead magazine-numbers an author's not unpardonable vanity..."   Fiction Pages 272

☐ **Life of David Crockett** by *David Crockett*   ISBN: *1-59462-250-7*   **$27.45**
"Colonel David Crockett was one of the most remarkable men of the times in which he lived. Born in humble life, but gifted with a strong will, an indomitable courage, and unremitting perseverance...   Biographies/New Age Pages 424

☐ **Lip-Reading** by *Edward Nitchie*   ISBN: *1-59462-206-X*   **$25.95**
Edward B. Nitchie, founder of the New York School for the Hard of Hearing, now the Nitchie School of Lip-Reading, Inc, wrote "LIP-READING Principles and Practice". The development and perfecting of this meritorious work on lip-reading was an undertaking...   How-to Pages 400

☐ **A Handbook of Suggestive Therapeutics, Applied Hypnotism, Psychic Science**   ISBN: *1-59462-214-0*   **$24.95**
by *Henry Munro*   Health/New Age/Health/Self-help Pages 376

☐ **A Doll's House: and Two Other Plays** by *Henrik Ibsen*   ISBN: *1-59462-112-8*   **$19.95**
Henrik Ibsen created this classic when in revolutionary 1848 Rome. Introducing some striking concepts in playwriting for the realist genre, this play has been studied the world over.   Fiction/Classics/Plays 308

☐ **The Light of Asia** by *sir Edwin Arnold*   ISBN: *1-59462-204-3*   **$13.95**
In this poetic masterpiece, Edwin Arnold describes the life and teachings of Buddha. The man who was to become known as Buddha to the world was born as Prince Gautama of India but he rejected the worldly riches and abandoned the reigns of power when...   Religion/History/Biographies Pages 170

☐ **The Complete Works of Guy de Maupassant** by *Guy de Maupassant*   ISBN: *1-59462-157-8*   **$16.95**
"For days and days, nights and nights, I had dreamed of that first kiss which was to consecrate our engagement, and I knew not on what spot I should put my lips..."   Fiction/Classics Pages 240

☐ **The Art of Cross-Examination** by *Francis L. Wellman*   ISBN: *1-59462-309-0*   **$26.95**
Written by a renowned trial lawyer, Wellman imparts his experience and uses case studies to explain how to use psychology to extract desired information through questioning.   How-to/Science/Reference Pages 408

☐ **Answered or Unanswered?** by *Louisa Vaughan*   ISBN: *1-59462-248-5*   **$10.95**
Miracles of Faith in China   Religion Pages 112

☐ **The Edinburgh Lectures on Mental Science (1909)** by *Thomas*   ISBN: *1-59462-008-3*   **$11.95**
This book contains the substance of a course of lectures recently given by the writer in the Queen Street Hall, Edinburgh. Its purpose is to indicate the Natural Principles governing the relation between Mental Action and Material Conditions...   New Age/Psychology Pages 148

☐ **Ayesha** by *H. Rider Haggard*   ISBN: *1-59462-301-5*   **$24.95**
Verily and indeed it is the unexpected that happens! Probably if there was one person upon the earth from whom the Editor of this, and of a certain previous history, did not expect to hear again...   Classics Pages 380

☐ **Ayala's Angel** by *Anthony Trollope*   ISBN: *1-59462-352-X*   **$29.95**
The two girls were both pretty, but Lucy who was twenty-one who supposed to be simple and comparatively unattractive, whereas Ayala was credited, as her Bombwhat romantic name might show, with poetic charm and a taste for romance. Ayala when her father died was nineteen...   Fiction Pages 484

☐ **The American Commonwealth** by *James Bryce*   ISBN: *1-59462-286-8*   **$34.45**
An interpretation of American democratic political theory. It examines political mechanics and society from the perspective of Scotsman James Bryce   Politics Pages 572

☐ **Stories of the Pilgrims** by *Margaret P. Pumphrey*   ISBN: *1-59462-116-0*   **$17.95**
This book explores pilgrims religious oppression in England as well as their escape to Holland and eventual crossing to America on the Mayflower, and their early days in New England...   History Pages 268

www.bookjungle.com email: sales@bookjungle.com fax: 630-214-0564 mail: Book Jungle PO Box 2226 Champaign, IL 61825

		QTY
The Fasting Cure by *Sinclair Upton* In the Cosmopolitan Magazine for May, 1910, and in the Contemporary Review (London) for April, 1910, I published an article dealing with my experiences in fasting. I have written a great many magazine articles, but never one which attracted so much attention... *New Age/Self Help/Health Pages 164*	ISBN: *1-59462-222-1* **$13.95**	☐
Hebrew Astrology by *Sepharial* In these days of advanced thinking it is a matter of common observation that we have left many of the old landmarks behind and that we are now pressing forward to greater heights and to a wider horizon than that which represented the mind-content of our progenitors... *Astrology Pages 144*	ISBN: *1-59462-308-2* **$13.45**	☐
Thought Vibration or The Law of Attraction in the Thought World by *William Walker Atkinson*	ISBN: *1-59462-127-6* **$12.95** *Psychology/Religion Pages 144*	☐
Optimism by *Helen Keller* Helen Keller was blind, deaf, and mute since 19 months old, yet famously learned how to overcome these handicaps, communicate with the world, and spread her lectures promoting optimism. An inspiring read for everyone... *Biographies/Inspirational Pages 84*	ISBN: *1-59462-108-X* **$15.95**	☐
Sara Crewe by *Frances Burnett* In the first place, Miss Minchin lived in London. Her home was a large, dull, tall one, in a large, dull square, where all the houses were alike, and all the sparrows were alike, and where all the door-knockers made the same heavy sound... *Childrens/Classic Pages 88*	ISBN: *1-59462-360-0* **$9.45**	☐
The Autobiography of Benjamin Franklin by *Benjamin Franklin* The Autobiography of Benjamin Franklin has probably been more extensively read than any other American historical work, and no other book of its kind has had such ups and downs of fortune. Franklin lived for many years in England, where he was agent... *Biographies/History Pages 332*	ISBN: *1-59462-135-7* **$24.95**	☐

Name	
Email	
Telephone	
Address	
City, State ZIP	

☐ Credit Card   ☐ Check / Money Order

Credit Card Number	
Expiration Date	
Signature	

Please Mail to: Book Jungle
PO Box 2226
Champaign, IL 61825
or Fax to: 630-214-0564

ORDERING INFORMATION

web: www.bookjungle.com
email: sales@bookjungle.com
fax: 630-214-0564
mail: Book Jungle PO Box 2226 Champaign, IL 61825
or PayPal to sales@bookjungle.com

Please contact us for bulk discounts

DIRECT-ORDER TERMS

20% Discount if You Order Two or More Books
Free Domestic Shipping!
Accepted: Master Card, Visa, Discover, American Express

www.ingramcontent.com/pod-product-compliance
Lightning Source LLC
Chambersburg PA
CBHW081329040426
42453CB00013B/2353